Net Wise

SAFE INTERNET USE FOR
THE ONLINE CHRISTIAN HOME

DOUG LASIT

Published by City Bible Publishing
9200 NE Fremont
Portland, Oregon 97220

Printed in U.S.A.

City Bible Publishing is a ministry of City Bible Church and is dedicated to serving the local church and its leaders through the production and distribution of quality restoration materials.

It is our prayer that these materials, proven in the context of the local church, will equip leaders in exalting the Lord and extending His kingdom.

For a free catalog of additional resources from City Bible Publishing please call

1-800-777-6057 or visit our website at www.citybiblepublishing.com.

NetWise

© Copyright 2002 by City Bible Publishing

All Rights Reserved

International Standard Book Number: 1-886849-96-X

NetWise

Introduction

One Click of the Mouse

Every time it happens, it's like a blow to the gut. If you are a parent, mentor, or youth leader and a young person comes to you with a problem in pornography from which he or she cannot break free, you know the feeling-it hurts deeply. You wonder when and where he or she saw it for the first time, and you wonder if you could have done something to prevent it. You also realize how hard it is to defeat.

Pornography, the most obvious peril of web browsing, is not the only cause for concern. There are thousands of shocking sites on hate, crime, human sexuality, and every other topic imaginable, and such sites receive tens of thousands of "hits" every day from America's youth.

While the Internet is used for education, information, and communication and has become a valuable and integral part of most of our lives, every parent, youth pastor, and teacher needs to know that the Internet is also the leading access point to inappropriate material today. The good and the bad are always linked together. In essence, a young person's life can be changed with one click of a mouse, accidental or otherwise.

No Fear

I am in no way trying to instill in you, as a parent or youth worker, fear of the Internet-quite the opposite. The Internet, the information super-highway, is the greatest technological achievement of the past century. It has ushered in a marked,

We must remember, however, that what is *amazing* is also *attractive*, and what is *attractive* is not always *innocent*.

instantaneous cultural shift. Understanding this shift takes both effort and education.

Many of our daily routine activities can now be accomplished from a desktop at home or from a laptop anywhere. Shopping, banking, communicating, and making dinner reservations can all be done in a microsecond of what it would have taken ten years ago. Do you remember those old sci-fi movies in which people could see each other on screen as they talked over computer networks instead of phones? In my household, we are now planning to buy our first web camera so that we can see and talk to extended family on different coasts at the same time. Amazing.

We must remember, however, that what is *amazing* is also *attractive*, and what is *attractive* is not always *innocent*. Are you willing to be educated in this technology for the sake of preserving the innocence and purity of your children?

The Internet is like a knife. In the hands of a chef, it can be an important instrument. In the hands of a criminal, it can be a very dangerous weapon. In the hands of a young or immature person, it can be a mistake waiting to happen. We caution our children never to run with anything sharp in their hands, carefully warning them of the danger: "This knife is not a toy." So it is with the Internet. We as Christians, parents, and leaders have a responsibility to understand, guide, and protect our families into safe, educational, and enjoyable Internet use in our homes and offices. We must be *NetWise*.

The Goal

The goal of this booklet is to provide *simple assistance* for safeguarding the home or office in the area of Internet use. The tools provided in this booklet are guided by important principles for protecting your family. Simply read through *The NetWise Family* as a whole, and then return to the specific sections that apply to your individual needs. The motivation to make simple changes in how you use the Internet should be fueled by principle and not bad experience. However, if someone in your household has already been exposed to dangerous material on the Internet, this booklet can also help you understand why and how to respond. This booklet is simply a tool to help you and your family enjoy and safely utilize one of the greatest inventions of our day, the Internet.

Understanding the Problem

Pornography is like terrorism—it hits you at home.

Pornography is like terrorism-it hits you at home. The days when your children had to purposely go looking for pornography are over. If you have the Internet in your home, chances are that you have already dealt with e-mail, junk mail, or accidental access to sites containing some pornographic material or other issues that would be detrimental to your home environment.

In the last ten years, with the explosion of the Internet, there has also been an exploding number of young people with an addiction to pornography. This problem affects not just young people, but anyone of any age who stumbles across it-dads, moms, brothers, sisters-everyone is vulnerable.

In ten years of working with young people, I have never seen such a drastic shift in one area of youth culture. Young people have been blanketed with pornography, both hard and soft. The Internet has made access to such material as easy as using the phone. All it takes is a little curiosity, combined with a little unpreparedness, and the result can be catastrophic in someone's life.

I recently spoke to a group of three hundred young people. In that meeting alone, more than one hundred identified themselves and asked for prayer because they had seen or experimented with pornography. As someone who speaks to and works with thousands of young people annually, I can tell you that this is not the exception, but the norm. Youth culture has made a shift!

- At the start of the 90s less than 2% of Americans used the Internet. In 2001 Internet use had climbed to 57%. In just ten years, more than half of all Americans have started using the Internet in some fashion[1]. Could all of America's

282 million people be online ten years from now? Here are some additional statistics[2]:

- 41% of all teenagers use the Internet every day.
- Only 9% of all teenagers say that they never use the Internet.
- 46% use it for chat rooms.
- 64% use it for music and videos.
- 35% use it to make new friends.
- 42% use it to maintain existing relationships.

❑ According to the Yankelovich Partner Poll, 44% of teen Internet users had seen X-rated web sites[3].

❑ 79% of teens who access porn sites do so from their school computers[4].

❑ A study by Net Value, an international Internet measuring company in Paris, found that if given the freedom, kids would indeed go to porn sites[5]. The facts they found:

- 27.5 % of teens younger than 17 had visited adult sites in the last month. (This is 27.5 % of all teens, not just boys.)
- 21% of teens accessing porn were 14 or younger.
- 40% of porn visitors were girls.
- Once on porn sites, kids spent 65% more time there than on game sites.

❑ An online article stated[6]:

*In 1999, C-net declared that online pornography was the first consistently successful e-commerce product. According to the National Review Online, the industry brought in an estimated $8 billion in 2000. In addition, more than **200 new porn sites flood the Web every day.***

Anyone who has ever played sports knows that one of the best ways to defeat the opposing team is to know what plays it has in its playbook. Coaches send scouts to watch opponents play other teams, and players watch endless hours of opponent video footage in preparation for the big game. As a responsible parent or youth worker, you too must know what plays the other side might pull out of its secret play book. It is your job, Coach, to lead the team into victory. If every play that your opponent pulls on you is a surprise, you need to do more research. Do what I have heard from many coaches over the years: "Get your head in the game!"

As Jesus said in Matthew 10:16, *"I am sending you out like sheep among wolves. Therefore be as shrewd as snakes and as innocent as doves."* Today's world of technology provides the devious with multiple ways to trap young people through visual snares. It is imperative that we remember that our children begin as blank slates, but the nature of an impure world is to defile the pure. Our goal is to remove opportunities for the enemy to infiltrate our homes and entice our children.

Here are some of the most common ways that that our children can be ensnared through the computer:

❏ Your child or teenager may go looking for pornographic or other harmful sites on the Internet.

❏ A friend or visitor with an addiction may access pornographic sites from your computer without your knowledge. Afterwards, you may begin to receive junk mail or advertisements from companies linked to sites visited.

❏ Someone may send you an e-mail message that has pornography connected with it.

❏ You or another family member may fill out a questionnaire or enter a drawing (online, in a mall, etc.), and your personal information is shared within a corporation or purchased by another company. You then start receiving junk e-mail or mail to your home containing inappropriate material.

❏ When looking for a particular web site, you may confuse domain extensions, such as .com and .org, and may accidentally access a pornographic site. We call these "shadow sites." (In my city, the web site for the airport has a shadow site, and if the wrong last three letters are used, the resulting site is a surprise. Domain extensions and their proper use are covered in the glossary.)

❑ You or another family member may log on to a web site, thinking that it is something else (like weather, sports, etc.), and it turns out to be a pornographic site.

❑ While doing an Internet search, the key word that is used may also key in on some pornographic sites. At these moments, whoever is doing the search has a choice to make right away.

1. Core Issues

Responsibility

The problem we are facing is not a difficult one to understand. We must wrestle with these two issues: 1) *how* do we fix the problem, and 2) *whose* job is it to fix the problem? This present age has heightened the level of responsibility for pastors, parents, and leaders. Though most parents are constantly playing catch-up with their Internet-savvy teenagers, they are still responsible for how their computer is used. Parents have the primary responsibility to cover and protect the home. The issue is not one of *understanding*, but of *responsibility*.

Our culture is in a constant state of denial and blame shifting. No one wants to be responsible these days. The state of the family today is a direct result of the lack of responsibility that has become so prevalent in society. "Family" has been redefined in our culture. Our culture now makes allowances for the irresponsible actions of "God-ordained" responsible family members. *Webster's Dictionary* has even changed its primary definition of "family" to include this sentence: *"Two or more people who share goals and values, have long-term commitments to one another, and reside usually in the same dwelling place."* This reads like a contract, strategically written with loopholes.

This is not the "family" that the Bible teaches us about. The biblical family is guided by absolutes and moral responsibility in the home. With the problems of American families today, with more than fifty percent of all marriages ending in divorce, our sense of responsibility has waned. People just seem to want out of their responsibilities. Whose responsibility is it, anyway? In your home, with your computer, it is *your* responsibility.

In today's world, even a small compromise hardly worth noticing to the unaware, irresponsible parent can have a life-long effect on a child. The Internet is the largest open door of small compromises that has ever existed.

Parents, we must recognize that it is our responsibility to protect and guide our home environment. There are no loopholes in parenting. This is true for single moms, single dads, parents who only have part-time custody, and traditional parents-it makes no difference! Please handle the computer responsibly for the sake of the children!

Preserving Innocence

In youth culture, to be innocent is not "cool." Yet the Bible tells us that to be innocent is to be godly, and innocence saves us from experiencing things that can cause us pain. It is important to remember that even though we are forgiven, we cannot "un-see" what we have seen. As parents and leaders, how do we preserve the innocence of our young people? We work at it!

> **The Internet is the largest open door of small compromises that has ever existed.**

While we do not want our children to be ignorant of culture and have untested spiritual muscles, we also do not want them exposed to some things too early, and other things at all. Our plan must include two components: 1) allowing them to grow, and 2) helping them to avoid mistakes or cultural traps.

What are cultural traps? They are the cultural snares that lure young people to look at, read, or experience things that are diametrically opposed to God's Word. These traps come in many forms. Some could be media- or entertainment-driven, while others could be pornographic links that come to your computer in the form of e-mail. These traps are designed to steal or stain the purity and innocence of our young people, and they have been set for any unsuspecting teenager who comes along. Those that set them have no feelings of regret or guilt for their actions or for the damage they cause in the lives of young people.

Examine these Scriptures and consider how they apply to our teens today:

> *"They shoot from ambush at the innocent man"* *(Psalm 64:4).*

> *"To the pure, all things are pure, but to those who are corrupted and do not believe, nothing is pure. In fact, both their minds and consciences are corrupted"* *(Titus 1:14-15).*

If the enemy can get your young person to look at graphic images or read something inappropriate, it will be easier to get him or her to look or read again. We have already mentioned that after looking at a pornographic site once, a young person will go back to that site 65% more often than other sites. This Scripture from Psalms is an appropriate reminder of the enemy's plot against young people: *"He lies in wait like a lion in cover; he lies in wait to catch the helpless; he catches the helpless and drags them off in his net"* (Psalm 10:9).

There is a well-known analogy that likens children to young plants in a greenhouse. Plants in a greenhouse experience a very controlled environment. Temperature and lighting are regulated, and they are fed specific foods for nourishment. Every type of plant is different, and every plant requires specific care. The controlled environment is the most important part of the plant's growth. Then, at the right time in the right season, the plant can be moved outside to finish its growth.

During one of the recent holidays, I experienced firsthand what can happen to a plant in the wrong environment. I left a poinsettia in the car for three or four hours while I visited some friends at their home. When I returned to the car, I found my beautiful poinsettia shriveled and close to death because of the extremely cold temperature. The effects of environment were very clear.

Similarly, the Internet has become a way for your son or daughter to be exposed to elements of culture before he or she is mature enough to make wise decisions. Often, we as parents are taken totally off guard! We may never suspect that we could deal with this in our own homes! We may have no idea that this could happen. In our innocence, we sometimes leave the back door open, and a cold breeze can blow through our greenhouse. In just a few moments, it can have a huge effect on our protected plants, our children. Preserving innocence should be in the heart of each parent, and each must do his or her own part in this process.

Wisdom in *accountability* is thinking ahead and putting in place a framework that can hold Internet users accountable *before* they use it.

Building Trust

In every area of today's culture, as it affects our children, we should use wisdom in accountability. *Wisdom in accountability* is thinking ahead and putting in place a framework that can hold Internet users accountable *before* they use it.

Your job, as a parent, is to provide your child with every opportunity for success. It is important for your young person to know that using wisdom in accountability is not an issue of *trust*, but an issue of *parental responsibility*. Decisions, such as where the computer will be located in the house, whether or not to use filters, how much time can be spent on the Internet, and who is responsible for checking web history and reading e-mail, are not issues of *trust*. These decisions are important because God has asked you to be responsible as a parent.

One of the best ways to help curb the negative potential of curiosity is to talk to your kids about the things they are curious about or things they may encounter.

Trust must be earned, but we must not set up our young people for failure, either. Parents and youth pastors often trust first, before creating the proper environment or framework of accountability for the child's success. Then, after the child has made a mistake, parents can't believe that their child would ever fail in this way. The unsuspecting parents end up being shocked and appalled, but because of their lack of wisdom in accountability, they themselves have contributed to the child's failure! Wisdom before opportunity would be a better parental approach.

Curiosity, as a powerful force of human nature, needs an outlet. One of the best ways to help curb the negative potential of curiosity is to talk to your kids about the things they are curious about or things they may encounter. Parents and youth pastors, be the outlet and talk to your kids! Be aware of the reality of curiosity and keep as many stumbling blocks out of the child's way as possible. With proper accountability, a child would have to go out of his or her way to find wrong or harmful material. This, now, becomes an issue of trust.

Deal with Intimidation

Many parents are somewhat intimidated by new technology. Though we all live in the technological age, some of us may not have found a great enough need to dive into the computer or Internet age.

Computer technology is not as intimidating today as it was just ten years ago, but like anything else, if we see no need to learn something new, we won't put forth the effort to do so. If you are just entering the computer world, or if e-mail has finally drawn you in, you have made a great first step! Now is the time to get past your feelings of intimidation and learn what you need to know to protect the other computer users in your home. Here are some tips to get you started.

❑ User Friendly Technology

Most of the technology that you will need is as easy to use as the phone book or as easy to follow as filling out a questionnaire or job application. Most software filters will guide you through the process of protecting your computer from Internet abuse. Simply answer the questions that the software program is asking and follow the instructions.

❑ Service Support

If you use the filtering technology that is provided by your ISP (Internet Service Provider), it is important to choose a provider that has good technical support access. You should be able to make a simple phone call to get the help that you need. ISP filtering can sometimes be complicated to use, and you may need to ask a few more questions from qualified support staff in order to set up the filters to meet your needs. One of the benefits, however, is that the controls cannot be changed from your home computer. This provides a little more protection overall because no one can change the settings on your computer without your knowledge. Therefore, this option may be more appropriate for homes with more computer-savvy users.

❑ Who is the Network Administrator in your home?

Do your children know more about the computer than you do? Every time you have a question about a computer issue, do you call for the teenager in your home? Your teenager might be a good source of technical support when you have a question about the computer or the Internet, but the responsibility for setting the boundaries for computer use will always be yours. You, not your child, should be the Network Administrator of your home.

I recently advised some parents to change the password on their computer filtering system. They agreed and responded enthusiastically, "We will do that immediately. We just need to ask our son what the current password is." Their son was sixteen, and because he knew more about computers, they let him set up the filtering system. This happens all the time.

Remember, in some ways the computer is like a language. The younger a child is first around it, the faster and easier it is for him or her to learn. No one is asking you to be a computer programmer, but if you have young children in the

R emember, in some ways the computer is like a language. The younger a child is first around it, the faster and easier it is for him or her to learn.

home, you should consider beginning the learning process immediately.

If you have children in the home, or if you desire to keep certain computer usage standards, you must learn basic skills to allow for computer accountability. Your child may know more than you do, but you need to have the authority and the knowledge to ask the right questions, know where to look for answers, and know who to call if you need help. Don't be afraid! And do not let your teens be the Network Administrators of your home.

Frameworks of Accountability

A "frame" gives structure, support, and internal focus to a thing or an idea. A "framework" gives external support for something that is being built.

Training and nurturing our young into the kind of people we want them to be is our parental focus. We are constantly focused on our children's internal value system, and we all have an idea of what kind of people we want our children to be someday. The practical ways that we shape their value systems make up the external framework. We are framing their character, and we use love, guidance, and discipline to get there.

A *framework of accountability* is the structural system that guides everyone who lives in your home and everyone who visits your home into safe and enjoyable Internet use. Keep in mind that it is common for a visitor who has a problem with inappropriate Internet use to browse on your computer when you are not looking. Your responsibility is to everyone who has or could have access to your computer.

Without consistency, accountability is just another good idea.

The first step should be to resolve that whatever framework you set up, you and your household are going to follow it. You must make a conscious decision to put forth the time and effort to make it successful. Consistency and planning make a framework possible. Without planning, you will never achieve the goal that you have set before your family. Without consistency, accountability is just is just another good idea.

Communication

One reason mistakes are made is that the lines of communication either do not exist or have broken down. Another good word for "mistake" is "pitfall." A "pitfall" is a big hole that people fall into because they didn't know it was there. Either they didn't ask about it, or no one warned them. The Internet must be discussed openly to avoid pitfalls.

Communication will play a vital role in the development of your children and in every situation that arises in your family. How you *communicate* will affect how you, as a family, and your children, as individuals, grow and mature. Communication is the key to building a sense of *community* in the home. More times than not, family communication is a reflection of the depth of family relationships.

What is a "sense of community" in the home? Do you have fun together? Do you talk openly with each other? Do your children know that their first line of defense is Mom and Dad? Do they enjoy bringing their friends into their family community, or do they seem to be drawn away from it? A meaningful sense of community is important for any child. The following steps will help build trust and community in your home if you follow them, and your home will be protected.

Here are three communication ideas that you can use to contribute to your framework of accountability. They are essential in maintaining a healthy Internet environment.

❏ Have a family meeting.

If you haven't done so already, I suggest having a family meeting to discuss Internet use in your home. It is wise to talk openly about its dangers, its positive uses, and your standards for the family computer. If you do this, everyone be on a level playing field. Everyone will understand the rules, and no one will be able to say that he or she "didn't know." Having family meetings will not only help in understanding the guidelines, but it will also give the family, as a whole, a goal and a standard in which to support each other. These experiences will strengthen the family.

❏   Ask for updates.

Ask those in your home if they have seen *any* strange e-mail, web sites, or disturbing material when they have been surfing the web. There is always a possibility that your particular filtering system is not doing its job for some reason. You *need* to know when something comes up on your computer that should not.

❏   Ask the tough questions.

Ask your children if they have seen *any* pornography *anywhere*. Get them to open up to you about the things they may have encountered in their journey though youth culture. If your child has encountered something along the way and he or she is willing to share it with you, this is good. You may also be able to estimate to what level he or she may be open to mistakes in the future.

This type of communication will build trust. If done in the right spirit, asking tough questions does not hinder your relationship with your kids, but rather, builds their sense of security and protection. This is what you want.

2. The Ten Commandments of Using the Internet

1) Never buy products or give credit card or other personal information online without Mom or Dad's supervision.

2) Never agree to meet in person anyone you have met or talked to online.

3) Never tell anyone online where you will be or what you will be doing at a certain time.

4) Never send a picture on the Internet or via regular mail to anyone you've met on the Internet without Mom or Dad's permission.

5) Never respond to anyone on the Internet who makes you feel uncomfortable, especially if he or she is rude or suggestive.

6) Always tell Mom or Dad about something you saw online, intentionally or unintentionally, that is upsetting.

7) Never give out your password to anyone without permission from Mom or Dad.

8) Be careful of anyone who offers something for nothing.

9) If you find yourself on a questionable site, close out of it, and tell your parents immediately.

10) Never pretend to be someone you are not on the Internet.

3. Safeguarding Your Home and Building Your Framework

The last place that our children should see inappropriate material for the first time is in our own homes. When this happens, it is because we have not taken the time to make improvements to our system of Internet accountability and family Internet education. In short, it is like leaving the doors of our homes open for thieves to walk in and take whatever they want. Our children's purity and precious godly innocence is worth more attention than it has been given in the typical American family environment. There must be locks on the doors and windows of our homes. When we go to bed at night, we usually check to see if the doors are locked, and we sleep in peace. This same simple principle should be used when improving Internet accountability.

Here is a framework to consider.

Set up the computer in a high visibility environment.

Never let your child have the Internet in his or her bedroom! Keeping the computer out in the open will help keep everyone who uses the Internet more accountable. Friends and visitors may not be as trustworthy as those who live in your home. It is important to keep your computer in a place where it will be more difficult for anyone to abuse computer privileges.

Set up the necessary filtering system.

To keep a safe computer environment for your children, you *must* utilize parental controls provided by your Internet Service

Provider or service software. Filtering systems will help keep online users from accessing inappropriate web sites or undesirable discussions, forums, and bulletin boards.

Have a family meeting.

Now that you are setting up the Internet in your home, it is time to have the family meeting discussed in the *Communication* section of this booklet. The purpose of this meeting is to communicate all of the expectations, rewards, disciplines, and potential problems that could result from using the Internet.

Pray and dedicate your computer.

When setting up the computer for the first time, consider praying over it and dedicating it to the Lord. Anything that can be used for good or for evil, like a computer, should be dedicated. Set a spiritual standard from the beginning for the use of any new item in your home. If your computer has already been in use for some time and mistakes have already been made, then you should do this as a new start and rededication.

Post the Ten Commandments of the Internet near the computer.

It would be wise to post the Ten Commandments of the Internet next to the computer. Remember the old adage, "Out of sight, out of mind." Posting the rules of Internet use right next to the computer will keep them fresh when they are needed most.

Ask periodic accountability questions.

In your family meeting, make it clear that you will periodically ask accountability questions, not because you question your children's actions, but because you are being faithful to your own responsibilities as adult and parent.

Do periodic accountability checks.

Schedule periodic checks of your web history, recycle bin, and e-mail. The more accountability that is in place, the more your computer users will feel protected, rather than violated, because it is a known family standard that these checks will occur. (For more information, refer to section 7, *How to Check Web History, Recycle Bin, and E-mail.*)

Reward and discipline accordingly.

It is very important to reward and discipline according to behavior. If your children show responsible Internet use, in today's youth culture, this is reason for reward! If they do not, it is important that you discipline accordingly, for *their own good.* (For more information, refer to section 11, *Reward and Discipline.*)

> **If your children show responsible Internet use, in today's youth culture, this is reason for reward!**

4. Six Common Excuses for Not Using Filters

"I have never had a problem before."

Again, what has happened in the past is not an accurate measuring stick for what may happen in the future. All parents who have not had filtering systems in place and whose children have not had an accident or incident with the Internet should consider themselves fortunate.

"Filters block out too much."

Many filtering programs have different levels of blocking. You can decide how intensely you want the filters to work or what type of sites you wish to block. The system will usually use key words to focus in on particular sites and block them. Many filters just log sites visited without blocking them.

"It's okay. I know how to check it."

The issue is not whether you know how to check which sites have been visited. The issue is whether you know how to prevent those sites from being visited in the first place. A false sense of security is often a front for irresponsibility or an issue of procrastination.

"I don't know how to set that up."

Don't let fear or lack of knowledge stop you from taking proper measures for responsible Internet use. A simple phone call or e-mail to technical support or a knowledgeable friend or a visit to an informative web site can help you through this process. (For a list of helpful web sites, refer to section 6, *Types of Filtering Systems*.)

"I keep forgetting to do it."

Don't let your child's first exposure to inappropriate material be the thing that causes you to remember to set up filters. Setting a weekly time to check your computer would be wise and would only take a few minutes.

"Filters don't work that well."

Often filters do not block out everything that you want blocked. To say that they do not work, however, is not true. You must first make sure that you have a good system in place and that your particular filtering system is looking for the right key words to block. Keep in mind that if a site is in a foreign language, the system will not be able to use key words to block material.

5. Types of Filtering Systems - How to Use Them

It is very important to use one of the following filtering systems when using the Internet. If setting up your filtering system seems a bit intimidating, let me put you at ease. If you are installing Internet service in your home, then you are already learning what you need to know, and setting up filters should be a breeze.

❏ There are three things that you should know if you are installing filtering software or subscribing to a system.

- The phone number of the company
- The web site of the company
- What you personally want from your system

❏ When you contact someone from the company, it is his or her job to walk you through the process of setting up your filtering system.

❏ Filtering systems have evolved in the last few years to become very user friendly. Here are some of the services that your system will perform for you:

- Log most, if not all, Internet activity
- Block access to adult sites
- Rate sites for you according to their pornographic, violent, profane, militant, or cultural content
- Set the time of day that you want each individual in your home to have access to the Internet
- Keep a record of all the sites that have been looked at by each individual in your home according to his or her individual password

Blocking/Filtering Software

There are several software programs that can help you, as a parent, more successfully control the Internet content that is available to your children. These are software programs that are very simple to implement. Most walk you through the process step by step, so that even the most inexperienced computer user can figure them out. Simply log on to the company's web site and follow the directions that it provides. Here are some examples:

- Cyber Patrol (http://www.cyberpatrol.com)

Surf Control, Cyber Patrol Division

1900 West Park Drive, Suite 180

- CyberSitter (http://www.cybersitter.com)
- CyberSnoop
  (http://www.pearlsw.com/csnoop3/snoop.htm)
- Integrity Online (http://www.integrityonline.com)

Online Services/Internet Service Providers

Another option for parents wanting to control online content is to sign up with an Internet Service Provider that restricts access to sites inappropriate for children. Some ISPs are geared toward family access and provide mechanisms that restrict children's Internet use. Some examples would include:

- AOL (http://www.aol.com) - If you are an AOL member and would like to set restrictions for Internet browsing, go to keyword PARENTAL, choose the screen name to restrict, click on TEEN or CHILD ACCESS, and follow the online instructions.
- CleanWeb (http://www.cleanweb.net)
- Family's Choice Internet (http://www.familyschoice.com)
- Integrity Online (http://www.integrityonline.com)
- MSN (http://www.msn.com) |
  P.O. Box 26897
  Salt Lake City, UT 84126
  (800) 386-5550

- Mindspring (http://www.mindspring.com/content/family)
- Prodigy (http://www.prodigy.com) - Prodigy recommends that its members download CyberPatrol software and use it in conjunction with their children's use of the Prodogy service.

6. How to Check Web History, Recycle Bin, and E-mail

Checking History - Internet Explorer

On the toolbar, select the HISTORY button . The History bar appears, containing links for web sites and pages visited in previous days and weeks. In the History bar, select a week or day that you want to view, select a web site folder to display individual pages, and then select the page icon to display the web page. To sort or search the History, select the arrow next to the VIEW button at the top of the History bar.

Tip: A quick shortcut that works with both Internet Explorer and Netscape browsers for checking web history is to press the CTRL key and then "H."

Checking History - Netscape

Open the Communicator menu, choose TOOLS, and then select HISTORY. To view a page, double-click its line on the list.

Tip: A quick shortcut that works with both Internet Explorer and Netscape browsers for checking web history is to press the CTRL key and then "H."

Checking the Trash

On the desktop, double-click the Recycle Bin (it looks like a trash can). Select the file or shortcut that you want to retrieve. On the File menu, select RESTORE. If you restore a file that was originally located in a deleted folder, the folder is recreated, and then the file is restored in the folder. To open a file that is in the Recycle Bin, drag the icon onto the desktop, and then select it. To retrieve several files at once, hold down the CTRL key, select each file you want to retrieve, and then select RESTORE on the file menu.

Mac Users

In Explorer: Look to the left-hand side of the screen and click on the "History" button. Then follow the directions.

In NetScape: Open 'Netscape' and select 'Communicator'. Select 'Tools' and then 'History'.

7. Isolation

Would you let your fifteen-year-old daughter be alone all night with a boy in her bedroom? Would you let your fifteen-year-old daughter stay up all night and talk to a boy on the phone in her room? The obvious answer is no!

The Internet offers a number of private environments where a young person can have the feeling that he or she is hiding away from everyone and can let down his or her guard. The Internet involves three of the five senses, sight, touch, and even sound, making it that much more inviting and appealing. When teenagers *would* not be so tempted to stay on the phone all night long, they would be tempted to stay on the Internet. This is one reason that I recommend that a teenager *never* have Internet access in the privacy of his or her own bedroom.

> **T**he Internet offers a number of private environments where a young person can have the feeling that he or she is hiding away from everyone and can let down his or her guard.

I once read a Calvin and Hobbs cartoon in which the two were standing outside, enjoying a beautiful night under the stars. Hobbs said, "When I ponder the mysteries of the universe, I feel so insignificant." Calvin replied, "Yeah, that's why I stay inside and play with my appliances."[7]

Technology has provided one of the most intense ways to "zone out" that has ever been invented, the Internet. There should be a balance to how much a child is able to surf or communicate on the Internet.

Watch for signs of isolation.

Because of the Internet's boundless potential for exploration, infinite knowledge, multimedia, and yes, even relationships, young people can very quickly become isolated and spend excessive amounts of time at the computer. The average teenager can spend anywhere from ten to fifty hours per week in multimedia engagement. Just five years ago, the majority of teenagers' recreational time would have been spent watching television, but now many of these hours have shifted to the Internet. When you add music, movies, and video games, a young person can spend an incredible amount of time being socialized by the media culture.

The dangers of spending too much time in isolated environments:

❏ Too much isolated time can hinder young people's ability to communicate feelings and struggles with others in a productive, relational, verbal environment.

During times of discipline or discussion, a child who has excessive amounts of non-verbal time with a computer or television can have difficulty opening up. It is important to teach our young people the importance of talking and expressing feelings and emotion. How can we assess or validate their feelings if we never hear them? This lack of communication can be a side effect of excessive isolated environments.

> Too much isolated time can hinder young people's ability to communicate feelings and struggles with others in a productive, relational, verbal environment.

❏ Young people learn to express themselves with others in nonverbal, rather than verbal, communication.

Turning a head, walking away, making contorted faces, or showing visible frustration without verbal communication are all examples of some of the obvious and intentional forms of nonverbal communication that could, over time, become a byproduct of spending excessive amounts of time in isolated environments. Young people may be trying to communicate things to you and may believe that they are doing so successfully. However, because they are communicating through their obvious non-verbal demeanor, you are left to interpret their actions. Without an interpreter, you will most likely misread what they are trying to communicate.

A great way to counteract this problem and rebuild verbal communication is to play interactive games with multiple players. You can also try playing non-media-oriented games that require family interaction. Additionally, consistently encouraging verbal communication with young people will help then learn. Don't just settle for the one-word answer, but rather, try to get an answer that explains or elaborates.

❑ Because young people can hide their identity on the Internet, they can explore, fantasize, create, and cultivate new identities without anyone ever knowing.

Because young people can hide their identity on the Internet, they can explore, fantasize, create, and cultivate new identities without anyone ever knowing.

One of the dangers of spending too much time on the Internet is that curiosity and opportunity will ultimately lead to decisions. Through the Internet, a young person can explore relationships, browse information, read others' conversations, assume imaginary identities, and fantasize openly with someone else about sexual experiences (known as "cyber-sex"). When a young person begins doing these things, he or she progresses to the next stage-deception. The young person does not want anyone to find out about his or her online behavior, and like pornography, without exposure and accountability, deception begins to pull him or her deeper into its clutches, and it becomes harder to break. Once deception has set in, the problem is much more serious than just a mistake of curiosity gone bad.

❑ Repetition can affect thought life.

Without a doubt, today's spiritual battle is a battle of the mind. This is especially true with computer and video games, where the experience is repetitive and non-verbal. Philippians 4:8 says, *"Finally, brothers, whatever is true, whatever is noble, whatever is right, whatever is pure, whatever is lovely, whatever is admirable-if anything is excellent or praiseworthy-think about such things."* Mental repetition can be positive if you are contemplating the right things. However, the result of repetitious negative thoughts is the old adage, "Garbage in-garbage out." Excessive and repetitive amounts of violence through video games and movies have proven to have a negative effect on the core of a person's thought life.

❑ Young people can be hindered in their ability to develop healthy friendships with others their own age.

Some young people have a tendency to be isolated and spend a lot of time on their computers or online. They need to be encouraged to do non-computer-related activities with other teens. If a media-focused habit is formed too early in the child's development, he or she can miss out on developing strong peer relationships.

Signs of too much isolated activity:

❑ Does your child seem to spend an excessive amount of time on the Internet?

❑ Have you noticed that your child does not spend as much time out with other friends lately?

❏ When your child is with his or her friends, do they spend the majority of time on the Internet or playing video games when they are together?

❏ Is the computer or video game the first thing your child goes to when he or she comes home from school? Is the purpose educational, relational, or something else?

❏ After using the computer, does he or she go straight in to his or her bedroom for the evening?

8. Children At Risk Online - A Word From the FBI for Parents

Computer sex offense, over the last ten years has become such a problem that Federal Government has given much time and energy bringing the protection of law to internet users and educating citizens on safe internet use. On the official FBI youth educational page (http://www.fbi.gov/kids/6th12th/6th12th.htm), you will find helpful material on computer-sex offenders and how to protect your children from them. Look at this introduction to their site. They wrote a letter to parents that we found encouraging.[8]

Dear Parent:

Our children are our Nation's most valuable asset. They represent the bright future of our country and hold our hopes for a better Nation. Our children are also the most vulnerable members of society. Protecting our children against the fear of crime and from becoming victims of crime must be a national priority.

For further information, please contact your local FBI office or the National Center for Missing and Exploited Children at (800) 843-5678.

Unfortunately the same advances in computer and telecommunication technology that allow our children to reach out to new sources of knowledge and cultural experiences are also leaving them vulnerable to exploitation and harm by computer-sex offenders. . . .

Louis J. Freeh, Director

Federal Bureau of Investigation

Their site goes on to provide some very helpful material on this subject and I would encourage parents to check it out.

Computer-Sex Offenders

Computer-sex offenders will use false identities to get teens to open up and then use the information they receive against them. You can become anyone, anywhere or any age that you want over the Internet. Sex-offenders will look for weaknesses in the children through chat room relationships and then try to get the child to compromise some bit of information about them selves. For instance: where they will be at a certain time, where they live, what school they go to, or a phone number. The offender can then use this information to lure a child into dangerous situation. A teen should never arrange a face to face meeting with someone they have met over the Internet.

The victimization of children can include the transfer of sexually explicit material over the Internet, or it can be as subtle as sexual conversation with a child. What is important to remember is that if you or any member of your family is approached or confronted with anything that is suggestive, sexual, obscene, or that you suspect is criminal, report it immediately to the FBI or the Center for Missing and Exploited Children.

What are signs that your child might be at risk online?[9]

❑   Your child spends large amounts of time online, especially at night.

❑   You find pornography on your child's computer.

- Your child receives phone calls from men you don't know or is making calls, sometimes long distance, to numbers you don't recognize.

- Your child receives mail, gifts, or packages from someone you don't know.

- Your child turns off the computer monitor or quickly changes the screen on the monitor when you come into the room.

- Your child becomes withdrawn from the family.

- Your child is using an online account belonging to someone else.

What should you do if you suspect?

- If you suspect that your child is communicating with a potential sexual predator online, communicate honestly and openly with your child. Ask him or her to reveal any and all information about what it is that you suspect.

- Share with your child the dangers and the strategies of a computer-sex offender.

- Review and monitor the web history on your computer, carefully check over your phone bill, read all e-mail, use and check Caller ID, and take any other necessary steps to discover important details and stop communication from sexual predators.

- Report what you find to your local FBI office (http://www.fbi.gov/kids/6th12th/6th12th.htm) or the National Center for Missing and Exploited Children at (800) 843-5678.

9. What Do You Do If You Find That Your Child Has Been Accessing Pornographic Sites?

Talk through the issue with love and support.

If you find that your child has been accessing inappropriate sites, you must talk through the issue with him or her completely before you make any quick decisions. It is important to know how long this has been going on, whether or not the Internet is the only access point to pornography that the child has been using, and how he or she feels about what he or she has been doing. You need this information to help in your decision-making. Always show love and hope the midst of dealing with an issue that involves discipline.

Establish a system of accountability.

The key to freedom in the area of pornography, besides the determination of an individual to make right choices, is accountability. By accountability, I mean setting aside a weekly time with the young person for the purpose of discussing what he or she has seen, any possible mistakes that he or she has made recently, and any experiences that may have taken place during the week. Without accountability, there is no outside framework to hold together the work that is happening in the young person's life.

Apply the Word of God.

As a Christian, I believe that there is power in the Word of God. It is important to apply to the situation Scriptures that give vision and direction as well as provide accountability.

Pray with strategic, accurate prayers.

Pray that the young person's mind would be renewed and that the Word of God would prevail in his or her life.

Prayer is an important part of breaking any bondage. Pray specifically for the problem. Pray that the young person's mind would be renewed and that the Word of God would prevail in his or her life.

Consider removing the Internet from your home.

This should be a "no-brainer" for any parent who cannot control how the home computer is being used and for any young person who is not responding to discipline and accountability. The cost of losing the Internet is minimal when compared to the cost of losing purity.

10. Reward and Discipline

Because many parents do not yet recognize how important the Internet is to their children, they often overlook the influence that the Internet is having on their teens, and they erroneously fault the phone or the television. Some parents still think the telephone is the most treasured possession in a teenager's life. Not true! Taking away phone privileges may have been a viable option for moderate forms of discipline ten years ago. However, many kids today have cell phones and pagers, and those things that were once privileges are now a mainstay in teenagers' lives. Many parents still view the computer as an educational tool or a word processor that makes work easier, because that is all it was for many of us when we began. This is not the case any longer. The computer is the telephone, the movie theater, the school, the mailbox, the filing cabinet, the library, and the place where teenagers share pictures of their vacations and friends. Wrongly using the computer or Internet is no different than abusing car privileges or some other major facet of the teenager's existence. It only makes sense that there should be some logical disciplinary procedures for misusing such an important part of today's millennial home.

It only makes sense that there should be some logical disciplinary procedures for misusing such an important part of today's millennial home.

We should remember what the Bible says about discipline: *"Our fathers disciplined us for a little while as they thought best; but God disciplines us for our good, that we may share in his holiness. No discipline seems pleasant at the time, but painful. Later on, however, it produces a harvest of righteousness and peace for those who have been trained by it"* (Hebrews 12:10-11).

Discipline

Here are five disciplinary actions that parents should be willing to take at any time, depending on the severity of the problem and the way or means in which the computer privilege was abused. For example, if deception, manipulation, or covering up were involved, parents should take more serious disciplinary actions.

❏ Consider suspending Internet privileges for a period of time.

❏ Consider suspending Internet privileges indefinitely.

❏ Consider revoking other privileges for abuse of Internet privileges.

❏ Consider requiring higher levels of accountability and time restrictions for the computer.

❏ Consider taking the computer out of the home completely, especially in cases when pornography, deception, and lying are involved. Questionable, negative, or dangerous Internet relationships are more serious situations in which permanent Internet cancellation should be considered.

In addition to taking disciplinary action that is suitable to the nature of the offense, the way in which discipline is carried out is equally important. There are four things to always remember in a context of discipline:

❏ There must always be hope for the restoration of the child, and he or she must know that.

❏ The reasons for the discipline must be clearly understood.

❏ The discipline must fit the crime.

❏ Discipline without relationship will lead to rebellion.

Reward

Always reward children when they have done well. Rewards are not for the sake of spoiling children, but when they can successfully and wisely navigate the Internet with today's challenges and pitfalls, recognition is in order.

❏ Consider rewards when a child alerts you to something that he or she has discovered on the computer that could have been potentially harmful in your home.

❏ Consider rewards that have the whole family in mind.

❏ Consider rewards in non-computer-related areas that make sense in your family context.

❏ Consider purchasing a game of which you approve.

❏ Consider rewarding those who have made mistakes but are working their way back to a position of trust.

11. Conclusion

God has a deep burden for young people. God is calling us to pick up his burden, and care about the things that affect this generation. The Internet has a huge effect, and is an integral part of every day life for today's youth. With its many vast possibilities for education, communication, and recreation, it makes a wonderful tool in the home. As parents, pastors, and teachers we have a responsibility to create an environment where this tool can be used successfully. We must take time to safeguard our homes, schools and offices in order to save our young people from the serious pitfalls that would cause unnecessary pain.

The enemy would love to steal the destiny of any young person. He knows the potential and power that comes through living a life of purity. He has strategically tried to use the today's technology to trap young lives in lust, deception, and wrong relationships. We must be aware of his strategy, and teach our young people how to keep themselves from falling into these traps. These things will rob them of living the productive and fulfilling lives that God intended for them.

It is a spiritual battle, but it is practical things that will help us win. We must do the practical things to protect our families. Read the computer manual. Talk to your child in the middle of a busy day. It will take time, effort and energy, but it will be worthwhile in the end. Get online and enjoy!

Helpful Definitions

Broadband: Fast Internet, such as cable or DSL.

Browse: Casual surfing through web sites on the Internet.

Bulletin Board Systems (BBS): A place for anyone to post messages, have conversations, trade information, and read messages from others. It works just like a real bulletin board in an office or home. There is usually one person who acts as the systems operator (or the keeper of the bulletin board), and you must go through that person's computer to access the BBS. Your computer simply calls the system operator's computer on the Internet and accesses the board.

Chat: Conversation between users in a chat room with no expectation of privacy. Anyone in the room knows that all chat conversations are read by everyone. Some chat rooms do offer private rooms that two users can enter into and have a private conversation.

Commercial Online Service (COS): These are services that give you access to the Internet for a fee. Integrity, America Online, Prodigy, CompuServe, and Microsoft Network are examples of this. Often service is limited according to the packages available.

Cookie: A file with information about the user placed on the computer by a web site.

Domains: Virtual "realms" for web sites. The most common, .com (or dot-com), stands for commercial, .org for non-profit organization, .edu for education (schools and colleges), .gov for government, and .mil for military. These are the most common, but others exist.

Download: Receiving data on to your computer through the internet or software that you desire to be stored in your computer for your use.

DSL: Digital Subscriber Line - The high-speed use of telephone lines to transmit electronic information.

Electronic Mail (E-Mail): A function of BBSs, COSs and ISPs which provides mail service, not of real letters, but of letters and information coming to and from your computer. The letter is electronic, so what the letter consists of is not limited to typed text but can contain video, sound, and virtual elements of the electronic world. The sender can remain anonymous through his or her e-mail address. No one is required to use his or her name as an address. Anyone can use any address he or she wants, as in "nonameguy@mail.com."

File Sharing (*See Software, Peer-to-Peer*)

Filter: A system or program that screens what information and web sites can be accessible or inaccessible from your computer and can be provided through your COSs. You can also install one yourself with third party software. Certain key words or pieces of information on a web site are detected that tell your filter to deny access of that information to your computer. Filters protect children or office employees from the ability to view inappropriate material, accidentally or otherwise.

Firewall: A virtual "wall" of protection for your computer from hackers, viruses, etc. It can either be a physical component or a program.

Hardware: Your computer's physical components.

Home Page: The first thing that comes up when you open a web site. It is like the cover of a book. Also used to denote people's personal pages.

Instant Messages: Private, real-time text conversation between two users in a chat room. Popular programs include AOL, Yahoo, MSN, and ICQ.

Internet: All of the computers around the world connected together through telephones and fiber networks, creating a global network. Your computer connects to an internal or external modem and calls your service provider. Your service provider connects your computer to the Internet. (Also known as the "information super-highway.")

Internet Relay Chat (IRC): Real-time text conversation similar to public and/or private chat rooms on COS, but with much less accountability to moderators. IRC, due to its more dynamic nature, is renowned for illegal material.

Internet Service Provider (ISP): Examples of ISPs are Erols, Concentric, Earthlink, Teleport, and Netcom. These services offer direct, full access to the Internet at a flat, monthly rate and often provide electronic-mail service for their customers. ISPs often provide space on their servers for their customers to maintain Worldwide Web (www) sites. Not all ISPs are commercial enterprises. Educational, governmental, and nonprofit organizations also provide Internet access to their members.

Modem: The device inside (or outside) your computer that connects to the internet via the phone line.

Online: When your computer is connected to the Internet.

Peer-to-Peer Software (*See Software, Peer-to-Peer*)

Public Chat Rooms: Created, maintained, listed, and monitored by the COSs and other public domain systems. These are like big conference calls to anyone who wants to talk, but participants type instead of talking. These chat rooms are monitored by the systems operators for inappropriate language and illegal activity. Abuse of chat rooms can result in revoking user privileges. Chat rooms cover every topic imaginable, and some are monitored more than others, depending on the systems operators.

Secure Site: Used in e-commerce, it allows the individual the ability to give personal information, such as phone numbers, addresses, and credit card numbers, with the decreased possibility of someone else accessing and stealing that information. Although security technology is constantly improving, no private data conveyed via the Internet is 100% secure. Use discretion.

Software: Programs or applications that run on a computer.

Software, Peer-to-Peer: Becoming much more popular recently, this software initiates more of a direct connection from your computer to others' computers on the Internet. The "middle-man" of web servers, e-mail servers, newsgroup servers, etc., is largely bypassed.
Warning: These types of programs and their activities are difficult to monitor or "log" and may even expose your computer to more malicious content (hacking, viruses, etc.). Such programs include Mesh, Aimster, and Gnutella. (Also known as "file sharing" programs.)

Spam: Messages, usually e-mail, sent anonymously in large quantity. Also used to denote "junk e-mail."

Surfing the Net: Using your computer to look at web sites, looking at more than one at a time, going from one to another in search of information, etc.

Uploading: Sending data or files from your computer to another.

Usenet (Newsgroups): Like a giant bulletin board where users post messages and information. Each posting is like an open letter and is capable of having attachments, such as graphic image files (GIFs). Anyone accessing the newsgroup can read the postings, take copies of posted items, or post responses. Each newsgroup can hold thousands of postings. Currently, there are over 29,000 public newsgroups, and that number is growing daily. Newsgroups are both public and/or private. There is no listing of private newsgroups.
The difference between material posted on a web site versus a news post is not unlike the difference between putting something on your front door versus the bulletin board at the grocery store. Newsgroup posts offer a much higher level of anonymity, hence explicit and even illegal posts.
Warning: The anonymous and temporary nature of news

posts makes illegal material harder to monitor or regulate. (*See also "IRC."*)

Virtual: The experience of computer technology incorporating as many of the senses as possible (sight, sound, touch, etc.). The more real the experience, the more "virtual" the experience.

Worldwide Web: All the web sites in the world put together and made available online, like the largest library in the world. It opens instantaneous communication.

Notes

1   George Barna, Real Teens (Ventura,CA:Regal:2001), Page 32.

2   Ibid., Pages 31-38.

3   Yankelovich Partner Poll, Time, (May 10, 1999), Pages.

4   Newsday

5   USA Today, (December 19, 2000).

6   Emily Smith, "Do You Know What Your Teen Saw on the Internet Today?" Focus on the Family, http://www.renewingtheheart.com/articles/A0000713.html.

7   Bill Watterson, Calvin and Hobbes.

8   Taken from internet site http://www.fbi.gov/publications/pguide/pguidee.htm

9   Ibid.